" Mi Amor" Poetry

"Mi Amor"
Poetry

Jerry Hayes

" Mi Amor" Poetry

ISBN: 0-9824699-2-6
ISBN-13:978-0-9824699-2-7

" Mi Amor" Poetry

DEDICATION

"Mi Amor" Thank you for sharing your life, thoughts, secrets, and beauty with me.

Jo Hayes; who always had faith in me.

"Mi Amor" Poetry

CONTENTS

i

" Mi Amor" Poetry

ACKNOWLEDGMENTS

Anna F.- Photography

" Mi Amor" Poetry

CREATION

Pablito

If God created both Adam and Eve
You created sex and this I believe
Rare could a fantasy truly be so real
Until a man touches you and this he feels

If God created both heavens and the Earth
You created the meaning of sex and gave it birth
Rare could pleasures truly exist
Sex was created with our very first kiss

If God created the highest mountains and the deepest oceans
You created sex in a process of slow motions
Power, intelligence and beauty given to a woman incredible
Needing no other food for because only you are edible

If God created the fish, animals and the birds
You created sex and the legend was now heard
God decided that he needed to rest on the seventh day
You created sex as only a man now rests and prays

Bridges

Pablito

Waters running down, far from the north
Needed in this valley for a farmers worth
Sailing boats down flowing river's existing wide
Keeping people on separate banks of the opposite side

Far apart in their own little worlds
Never knowing of others existence can they find the pearls
Separated by many things in this life
Causing nations of people to start wars and increase strife

Hoping to build a bridge across everyday
Overcoming obstacles in many ways
Slowing driving peers deeper into water, day by day
Monument of love bridging the rivers for years to stay

Crossing over flowing waters that truly divide
Permitting others in their own little world should not hide
Differences of people who are different and always apart
Now giving them a chance at love, finding a new start

The Diamond

Pablito

Buried deep within the earth for millions of years
Bodies of suitors sweating blood and flowing tears
Seeking perfection and beauty that earth does not show
Waiting all around to see her shining with a special glow

Uncovered from the depths of the unknown world
Pressurized waters rising around in many twirls
Bringing to the surface so all around now can see
Radiating beauty sparkling and unlocked was the key

Strongest minerals from determined journeys she became
Never apologizing and never knowing others games
Precious and valuable the world wanted to possess
Only a very special diamond separates her others from the rest

You

Pablito

Loving the way that you are finding to live
Loving the way that to me, you will always give
Believing the many things you express and say
Living your life each and every single day

Enjoying the time that is spent with you
Enjoying the many things we find to do

Seeing in you the best from so close and near
Causes one to never have concerns or jealous fears
Joining now to that heart of your yearning soul
Spending time together, one young, becoming grey and old

Glittering Snows

Pablito

Falling waters, cascading from heavenly heights
Glittering winter snows coming during the night
Summer beaches warming the souls of people many
Living in a land that other countries call plenty

Smells of flowers, awakening our scents
Vulnerable feelings that lowers the emotional fences
Timbers of wood flickering in late night beach fires
Finding someone that you truly love and admire

Coming to this land and touching others' lives
Joys and heartbreaks wondering if our love will survive
Passions of soul that few experience or really know
Passions of the flesh, yearning inside and wanting more to sow

Moments in time happen each and every day
More moments come and then the next in a different way
Feelings from the heart much harder explain or say
Deep appreciation for you, forever and today

Coming Closer

Pablito

Watching her eyes that cannot deny
Deep colors resonating like summer skies
Playing music softly that one can hear
Nothing neither existing nor causing the slightest fear

Curious all the time as individuals can be
Wondering what happens and waiting to see
Secrets hidden deep in hearts of a youthful past
Enjoying moments, wondering how long they can last

Never possessing, like water in a babies hands
Seeking larger worlds and the finest of lands
Coming closer my lover, because it's not a sin
Coming closer my angel and now my friend

Passions of life that we already know
Passions of love and how you will show
Coming closer if only to feel my lips
Moments passing together, like two wandering ships

An Interesting Soul

Pablito

Deep inside hearts of the interesting souls ... searching her eyes for love
and understanding
Understanding as she always wanted the answers for her questions about
lost dreams
Dreams of happiness persisting in the face of issues encountered and
experienced
Experiences of two lives embracing that are not yet over completely
Completely day after day pretending there are no problems today
Today to be lived with the roles each given
Given dreams to become their own reality
Reality wishing for days of supine joy
Joys, staying longer than a moment
Moments shared and never revealed
Revelations, thoughts, feelings
Feeling cherished
Cherishing
Cherishing You
You today, Now
Now seems all mine
Mine hoping there is more
More is less when not there
There are only lonely thoughts of you
You walking into my life and reviving me
 Me wondering how a soul connects to another soul
Souls feeling alone yet yearning to be closer to another
Another heart, another soul, another mind, each with its on questions
Questions about self or even questions about the world that surrounds us
Us understanding as she always wanted the answers for her questions
about lost dreams
Dreams inside hearts of the interesting souls ... searching her eyes for love
that is so deep

Tender Lips

Pablito

Eyes radiating brightly from across the table
Sharing moments of past experiences two are able
Billions and billions of stars, suns, moons and lights
Struggles with lust and feelings, you and I start to fight

Wondering how these moments can even exist
Knowing do I that no man could really resist
Beauty that speaks loudly and deeply from within
Beauty that speaks when you are forced to pretend

Loving easy, with warm fires and the peace
Fleeing clothes and naked bodies finding gentle release
Poetry written that might someday find a way
Memories of the minds in eternity, which are special today

Love and loving never really hard to do
Many men around the world desiring you
Forever memories of such hidden delight
Touching such tender lips, late into a romantic night

Sensual

Pablito

Walking into the room with burning scented candles
Breathing smells of the candles on fireplace mantle
Playing music and moving slowly rhythms pounding musical beats
Burning logs in fireplaces and feeling each other's warmth and heat

Warm and safe feelings during these hours and moments tonight
Questions far distant about whether wrong or right
Aroma of the other person's body closer and sweet
Decisions make about where two together can meet

Conversations long and words of encouragement embraced
Pains and fears of the past all seemly now erased
Long legs and beauty possessed in all the right places
Classy and elegant attired in garments of white laces

Sensual is not just an act that can be played
Sensual is not easy women who just need to be laid
Holding of hands around two crystal glasses of Chianti wine
Sensual is more about all the moments shared together in time

After the Orgasm

Pablito

Making love is not just a silly game to play
Wanting only to be close to cuddle and then to stay
Raining like a hurricane or maybe a thunderstorm with snow
Afterwards, quickly is out the door that one has to go

Running away so quickly afterwards is what disgraces me
Desiring only a relationship to grow like a solid tree
Yearning so much for your pleasure and for your fun
Knowing afterwards that relationship is completely done

Great lovers know it's not just the orgasm that counts
But that act of pleasing continues after the dismounts
It's after the orgasm that really shows how one truly feels
After sex shows a woman if deeper emotions of love are real

"A glass of water can you get now for me"
"Honey, the air conditioner needs to be on 73"
After sex and a man has shown this biological seed
Shows a woman whether she is loved, used or just a sexual need

Jerry D. Hayes

"Do You Have Any "Regrets"

Pablito

"Regrets", do they live today inside of you?
Thinking about some of the things that we do
"Regrets" present and coming with the mornings light
Questions about whether actions were wrong or right

"Regrets" did they creep into the darkest night is sleep
Causing one to not sleep but slowly cry and weep
"Regrets", wishing that our actions never began
Pretending that there is someone else that you cannot stand?

"Regrets" did they make you think so differently today?
Walking around looking so distant and far away
"Regrets" about some things and reliving them inside
Working all day, I cannot tell what it is you hide

"Regrets" of choices that were made long ago
Feelings that once you had but you never did show
"Regrets" of worlds that you left long behind
Love of others and that you felt was far more kind?

"Regrets" might come and regrets might go
Emotions deep inside back then that you did not know
"Regrets" can live inside but regrets can also die
"Regrets" only survive when there are questions of "why"

Every Kiss

Pablito

Every kiss as sweet as any expensive gift
Seconds counted where there is no rift
Parting of lips every moment now counted
Worlds no longer matter as one in battle surrounded

Secrets lives now that one does begin
Feeling like every minute a giant win
Knowing someday that time will be gone
One does not really care if right or wrong

Precious times realizing that together we can be
Needing no one to tell us for only you can I can see
Every kiss brings inside him this type of thought
Every man's longing this type of kiss desirously sought

Stealing Time

Pablito

Imprisoned persons sitting in local jails
Wasting their lives in the smallest cells
Looking at walls and looking at few nails
No one to listen to problems and their stories to tell

Sick little children living in hospitals they only know
Restricted to their rooms with nowhere else to go
Cancers existing with bald heads and hair missing to show
Happy for moments because the years they will not know

Crying lovers on the phone all throughout the night
Deceived by men whose actions were not right
Once held in his arms so caring, warm and tight
Making efforts for hours to look pretty in his sight

Anticipating the moments in beautiful afternoon sun
Sitting in a restaurant waiting for someone to come
One person waiting and sitting there way to long
Seconds and moments alone listening to the music and songs

Time is a gift that one never really knows
Whether is it given in truth only later does it show?
Making decisions they hope will really make sense
Happiness or sadness to themselves they must convince

No guarantees of the exact quantities can we really plan
Stealing the seconds each day so hard to truly withstand
Not something that is easy to really understand
Time is the greatest gift given to man

The Safest Place

Pablito

Telling him my biggest secrets and feeling sure
telling me his secrets like a mysterious tour
Smiling at me, feeling now safe is my cure
Laughing and caring is how together we endure

Knowing a special feeling was a heavenly sign
Loving heart that was gentle and to me kind
Never feeling that every word was just a conquest plan
Knowing the heart of a woman but still he is all man

Wanting someone into my daily life
Passing each day without reasons or strife
Feeling more and more of a loving way
Causing me reasons to linger and stay

Choosing his words wisely, if then telling of what is wrong or right
Even when I'm wrong, he tells me I am beautiful in his sight
Accepting me, and never wanting him to be hurting of me
Knowing me, and the understanding that he sees

Playing and dancing all through the night
However things might turn out, it's still feels right
Yes, I am a beautiful woman who exits today
He is a beautiful friend, staying in my life until the end

Moments together sharing and making me smile
Silly fun, enjoying that I have not known for a while
Being together enjoying poured glasses of Italian wine
Trying not to be so worried about the future in these sensual times

A season or a lifetime, forever or just this one year
Time together not worrying about any of my deepest fears

Silent

Pablito

Words existing but are not being expressed
Feelings harbored deeply inside without much success
Moments lost because of misunderstanding thoughts
Seconds wasting and experiences for together two lovers sought

Hearing only the words expressed, but many are not spoken
Smiles across the face seeming to be her token
Upset inside she might really have been
Feelings of regrets of actions maybe a sin

Wanting to know just how she really felt
Seeking an answer before this freeze will melt
Closeness that once was enjoyed by two
Answers to the questions if he only knew

Extremely happy, steaming mad or even glad
Maybe a urging that somehow made her sad
Sharing the love of another is so hard to lose
Silence is such a powerful weapon for any woman to use

With Your Body

Pablito-

Slowly dropping now to my knees
Hoping only to be giving to you to please
Gentle touching on all the parts of your body
Wondering how God creates such a "hottie"

Lips so luscious and so very nice
This lover would feel your loving entice
Breasts that enjoy a sucking embrace
Moments of a night one should not erase

Hands that are covering all of your flesh
Coming together bare two bodies mesh
Seeking the closeness of hidden beauty
Forgetting of work and of all other duties

Exploring all of parts of your body that one does admire
Giving to you to fulfill your most basic desire
Physical pleasure that is lost in time
Smooth parts of your body radiate and shine

The Valley

Pablito

Years of living on the mountain and its slopes
Others existing in the valley of life and hopes
Wandering from time to time to the valley floor
Only to run away when life was uncertain and nothing sure

Looking at problems for a very distant view
Thinking those in the valley really never had a clue
Sitting on the high up mountain's side
Not facing all the truths, but a place to hide

The valley is the place we must learn to live
Living in the valley learning to others to give
Painfully emotions love can often be
Greater pain would loneliness in others to see

The Day After

Pablito

After being with you time short or long
Still listening to the music and many songs
Thinking about all the things spoken we say
Laugher and the times we just joke and play

Finding myself quiet at work the next day
No expressions and having a face of clay
What really going on within the depths inside
Thinking about you living with me by my side

Kissing your ear, back and shoulders
Reliving the moments over and over
Conversations with others seeming so contrite
Wanting to kiss you again the feelings to fight

The day after being with you all night
Everything seems perfect and incredible right
Feeling now that continues inside to live
Wanting more just to you. to give and give

Caring

Pablito

Caring about you is not some type of game
It's not about silly words or frivolous names
Not just an objective that needs to be gained
Not a woman who needs to be tamed

Caring about you and your previous child
Understanding all things graceful and truly wild
Caring about your health and finances to survive
Understanding those conditions that allow you to be alive

The Night Doubts Died

Pablito

Maybe the place was not the best
Needing better accommodations and a place of rest
Roses can blossom and bloom still late at night
Changes happening between lovers in morning light

Doubts existed in the back of my mind
Could God really be to me this kind?
Loving spirit deep inside of you each day
Caring and giving to me in just every way

Thankful for your views and life's insights
Thankful for the moments of pure delight
Asking myself questions about you and why
Finding answers in the night that doubts did die

La Rosa, Mi Amor,

Pablito

Grow my rose in so many different ways
Plenty of sunshine required every night and day
Rich and darken must be the soil
Providing the nutrients of the daily toils

Pouring on water that gives it life
Controlling the weeds that bring only strife
Pruning and trimming in the hands of the master
Guarding against insects and disease that brings disaster

Purity, innocence, silence, secrecy, humility is the white
Pink is "thank you", grace, for the most perfect of nights
Yellow means joy, gladness, friendship and delight
Promises of new beginnings those are perfect and right

Orange roses stand for enthusiasm and desire
Light pink is for sympathy and that one is admired
A Red rose is for love, beauty, courage and respect
Thorn less roses "love at first sight" one does not expect

You are my love that no one knows
You are my flower and you are my rose

Walking Around

Pablito

Walking around today much in a complete daze
Seeing the sunshine and yet seeing morning haze
Thinking all day but only about the night
Noticing how beautiful you exist in my sight

Walking around this morning seeming like a blank
Wanting to walk even if it's just down to the lake
Reliving the touch of every late night kiss
Even thinking about how much you are truly missed

Wanting to think about only you today
Wishing to go with you or you that one could stay
Always realizing how love should really be
Loving and giving to me examples of this love can see

Walking around being both happy and sad
Glad for your reunions growing up that you once had
Seeing the lad whose happiness brings you to life once again
But, sad for thoughts deep inside were you will have to pretend

Walking around but now finding the time to write
About the joy and pleasures shared though out the night
Poems may come easy or they might come slow
Loving you, I hope these poems will always forever show

Where

Pablito

Where do you go when you are sitting on a plane?
Sitting there thinking, not being able to explain
Traveling to a world so far away
Wondering if circumstances enable you to stay

Where do you go when you are sitting on the patio?
Questioning the decisions whether they were yes or no
Traveling to a country that you did not know
Creating a life inside when you were beginning to show

Where do you go when you feeling that life is not fair?
Gaining again that confidence to fight or dare?
Staring off into space with a faraway fazed
Being only occasionally shaken or dazed

Where do you go when you are really alone?
Questions and answers that are not known

Reveal

Pablito

Everything hidden close to me

Not trusting others inside what to see

All about faith, now all about the trust

All about luck, and not about lust

Revealing now everything for you

Revealing the truth and only to you

Wishes of mine now coming true

Wishes of mine about things we do

Special in the morning and special all day

Floating in space feelings of drifting away

Making me warmer and making me high

Feeling like laughing where once I would cry

...

Revealing the most tender places inside me

Hidden fears and concerns others will never see

Revealing the future each and every day

Whether I have to go and whether I can stay

When Beauty Smiles

Pablito

Lying quietly in glistening morning light
Sheets uncovering flesh now within my sight
Eyes closed pretending you are asleep but really awake
Reaching for just one touch of prefect breasts now make

Gentle kisses upon parts of your body, now I go
Beauty in ways that others truly will never know
Deeper thoughts and feelings of this lustrous beauty
Many roles to play and many obligations and duties

Lighting up rooms with the flashing of your smiles
Radiating for the moment and for thousands of miles
Like the largest diamond or most precious of things
Appreciation of the elegance that beauty does now bring

Beauty smiles this early morning in June
Having arrived so late with twinkling moon
Hopefully avoiding dangers and avoiding strife
Escaping to this secret place existing in her life

Listening To Your Heart

Pablito

Seeing something in the wake of your smile
Getting a notion about looks in your eyes for a while
Building a love but knowing that all love can fall apart
Pieces of your heaven how quickly can they turn to dark

Listening to your heart when she's calling for you
Listening to your heart there's nothing else you can do
Knowing never where you are going and reasons why
Listen to your heart before ever telling her goodbye

Sometimes you wondering if fighting is worthwhile
Precious moments lost in tides never able to even smile
Sweeping away and nothing is what it really seems
Feeling of belonging to you if only in your dreams

Listen to your heart and the little voice
Wanting to be heard among life's other noise
Not really able to find all the right words
Scents of magic, now the beauty that is heard

When love is wilder than the wind
Knowing the beginnings but never the end

Inside of You

Pablito

Exploring a world in many different places
Times remembered and times that were wastes
Special moments burned into my mind
Not always often and not even all the time

Growing older with each passing year
Growing wiser because of joys and for tears
Waters flowing down many rivers of life
Bridges crossed whether peaceful or strife

Sitting at lunch during the middle of the day
You came into my life never expecting to stay
Living your life in special and unique ways
Sometimes serious and sometimes wanting to play

Surrounded by your beauty and elegant grace
Living now and finding this amazing place
Even beautiful while sleeping is a delight
Sensual in the morning and even late at night

Finding this place and enjoying much to be
Where nobody knows and nobody can see
Stories they would tell if they only knew
This cherished place that is deep inside of you

Everyday

Pablito

Finding many things the same each day
Feelings and questions always similar in many ways
Rising to the glittering rays of mornings early
Up too late? Wondering if now you are surly?

Asking myself did you make it safely home?
Wondering if there is a message on my phone
Are you safe from dangers that always seem to lurk?
Has someone is your life gone crazy or a little berserk?

Each day begins with thoughts about the night
Thinking about conversations and what a delight
Memories and images coming into my sight
Even planning for battles that we might have to fight

Wanting to make sure that you are always protected
Never feeling in any way that you are rejected
Looking into your eyes and amazed at what I can see
Thankful every day for finding just an image of me

The Scent of You

Pablito

Warm glowing embers heating my heart
Memories of last night from ending to start
Flames of passion from the beginning to the end
Tangled flesh of two bodies thoughts now descend

Lightning striking distances both heaven and earth
Filling this emotional longing of insatiable thirst
Enjoying tonight closer than any two passing ships
Music arousing sensual movements of your hips

Sharing your feelings and much of your concerns
Creating a trust between lovers wanting each now the other yearns
A night fills the space after the absence of light
In the darkness of being together the givers delight

Aroused in the morning and missing you too
Enjoying the pleasures created by the bodies of two
Searching my bed, my shirts, my boxers I must do
Trying to find now even a slight faint scent of you

Leopard

Pablito

Roaming the earth late into the night
Causing other animals envy and fright
Roaring aloud to the shuttering of men
Never leaving tracks of where you have been

Sitting high above the world so you can see
Dangers approaching while you are resting in the trees
Greatest hunter of jungles this animal is the best
Queen of the forest you are greater than all the rest

Frustrations that mount that can turn into rage
You cannot exist if you are confined to a cage
Dying a death inside you never wants to face
Captivity of your soul you never want to taste

Hunting and mating, you are the jungle queen
Prey devoured before they notice or you have seen
Speed and power this creature has much
But rare is this animal that one can even touch

Breath

Pablito

Slowing taking a deep breath in my lungs
Letting air release as music plays and the songs are sung
Relaxing after being with you for an enjoyable day
Peaceful calm existing even after now being away

No worry or concerns about the world can I feel
Wanting only moments with you that as lover can steal
Feeling my own heart pounding strongly inside
Only the thoughts inside my mind must I continue to hide

Recent memories of the days and nights together
Touching your breasts and body as light as a feather
Slowing taking another breath again and again
With all my heart and mind protecting you, wanting to defend

Becoming the very breath that continues to inhale
Stories of love and caring to others wanting to tell
Realizing each day how love should really be
Breathing into my lungs the essence of just thee

Jerry D. Hayes

Addiction

Pablito

Spending the hours, months, minutes and years

Sharing the victories, struggles and occasional fears

Seeking the answers to direction or why there are tears

Drinking and inhaling of this substance consumed so near

Exuberances and highs experiencing at last

Finding a woman with intelligence and class

Injecting the substance deep into my flesh

Wondering if this drug is really some type of test

Day after Day not realizing existence of time

Walking on the beach as this sun only shines

Arguments and challenges encountered today

Planning on packing all my things and wanting to run away

Water for the body signaling the need or thirst

Drugs overdoses bringing the morticians and the local hearse

Every person can have a vice or a very strong need

Addiction to your love is what I now plead

Bridges To Far

Pablito

Traveling roads day after day and well into the night
Gone from the home with fading distant lights
Moving in directions down the long and winding road
Happening events that one has not to others even told

Leaving a house and getting into this aging car
Quickly having to pass bridges before going very far
Casting new plans while passing the swollen rivers, long and wide
Memories new created days and nights one does hide

Farther and farther from times once familiar one knew
Bridges crossed after another bridge asking what one should do
Turning the car around many times inside my mind
Roads traveled in the other direction seemed to be a sign

Rivers and obstacles overcoming one has to take
Bridges crossed and the decisions forced at times to make
Turning the car around can we go back to a point in time?
Bridges to far crossing and hoping life will be now loving and kind

Oceans

Pablito

Walking on the narrow path through life's little forest

Coming to a stop, if only for brief seconds to catch a rest

Nearby pond, seeing there swimming were many swans

If by magic, like beautiful fairies waving wanes

Walking out of forest trees into a wide open field

Finding a small cottage sitting on rolling hill

Opening a door, coming into this cozy little place

Finding oak table, with red wine, blessed with goodness and grace

Leaving this table, hearing the seagulls in the distance

Giving up to my desire and finding so little resistance

Standing on the shady shores looking out over blue sea

Feeling that urge that was so deep others could not see

Heading for vast oceans and wanting so much more

Stepping into cold waters and leaving this shore

Plunging into crashing waves and taking into my lungs ample air

Immersing and consuming myself into this ocean I dare

Breaking Dawn

Pablito

Frequently fantasizing making love to you
beneath the moon until early morning at two
On sandy beaches or atop hoods of a parked car
under night's brightest glowing evening stars

Intertwining two naked two bodies.... in my head
lying on the apartment couch or the nearby bed
atop a summer mountain's in Jackson Hole from dawn to dark
Even among the green trees in Dublin Park.

In medieval castles in faraway distant lands
maybe even in an elevator in busy Manhattan
Thinking maybe it could be either here nor there...
What about Bahamas' breathing the salty-sea air.

Staying at a hotel in ancient city of Milan
in the bed or maybe as two just trying to stand
mattering not where two lovers would be...
that wondering eyes may try to see

Being discrete but our bodies together that can weave
no traces of our intimacy shall be taken leave
resisting not the passion that between two lovers does arise
intoxicated by the delight of lustful surprise

Unveiling our mild-mannered seemingly normal disguise
Making love even at this moment does not seem wise
Passion having its own Himalayan snowcapped peak
roaring untamed fires untested lovers faithfully seek

Inside, outside, longing desires finding most anywhere
Glistening naked bodies that really just don't care
Human desire manifesting and growing ...never be withdrawn
Love's explosive yearnings having this breaking early dawn

Breathing In

Pablito

Breathing in these brief seconds and moments of time
Beautiful white beaches where the sun forever shines
Walking along sandy beaches and seeing swimming white fish
Capturing moments and images and making promises and a wish

Breathing in the precious minutes existing in our lives
Finding contentment, peace and not feeling any strife
Walking cobbled streets of these old historic towns
Laughing like children at a circus and being clowns

Breathing in the glasses of white wine over a Greek lunch
Reaching over calamari appetizers receiving your touch
Breezes flowing over the island from the night ocean air
Glances of people looking at your beauty, wanting you to stare

Breathing in images of morning suns rising in the east
Touching flesh as yearnings deep inside starting to increase
Lying in bed with arms wrapped around one another
Goose bumps developing over skin as you shutter

Breathing in summer's breaking dawns looking nearby palm trees
Passing tropical winds that send thousands of ships out to sea
Going around the island with many pictures we have taking
Memories in the present, while breathing in and making

Growing Old

Pablito

Facing and getting closer to that eternal great sleep
Radiating with your eyes, such beauty when you I would meet
Nodding softly by cold nights' warming fires
Reading slowly and dreaming of past desires

Many having loved your life of beauty and grace
Relinquishing the sorrows of your changing face
Loving your beauty were they with false love or true
Cherishing did one man the spirit deep inside of you

Longing again since I journeyed to distant stars
Bending down from the heavens and from distant Mars
Deeply sadden, that I was never able just with you to stay
Thinking sadly, how love had perished on that summer day

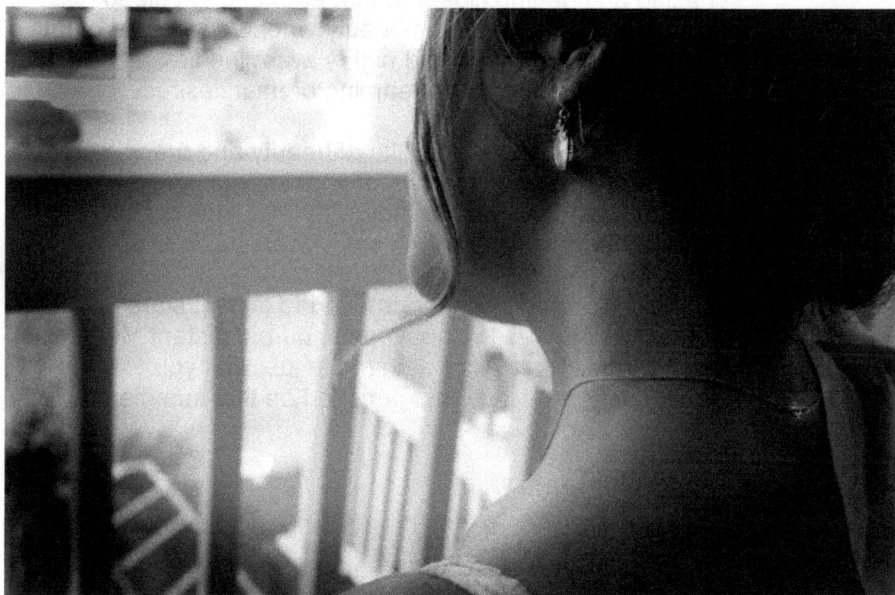

Marriage

Pablito

Being born together this day with you and forever more

Never parting at death nor on any distant shore

Being together with silent ideas that God really does exist

Coming closer to each as one in holy togetherness

Letting the winds of the heavens dance not between

Loving one another, making that bonds of love now be seen

Letting not a watery sea come between oceans of wandering souls

Filling each other's cup, letting all love to everyone show

Sharing loafs of bread until there is none more to share

Singing and dancing together letting smiles of joy now wear

Harmony of life like music being played as strings on a guitar

Giving hearts to each and never wanting to be separate too far

Pillars of the temple standing apart each be fair

Strength of the building together each does share

Tender hands of life containing each other's heart

Standing together letting life together now start

Saying Goodbye

Pablito

Never one wanting to say good bye

Never one wanting to show a tear or cry

Moments of parting bring great stress

After sharing passions now coming to rest

Conversations very late into many wine filled nights

Dancing together out of jealous others sights

Poetry filled lives that were by you inspired

Gazing eyes of so many others as you are admired

Saying goodbye I will never do

No giving up on love, no giving up on you

Hiding place of love living deep inside of me

All the world, may never find nor be allowed to see

Words, many words that have been spoken

Expressions of love that were never just a token

Hoping against hope that this is not the last

Believing that love is a future and not the past

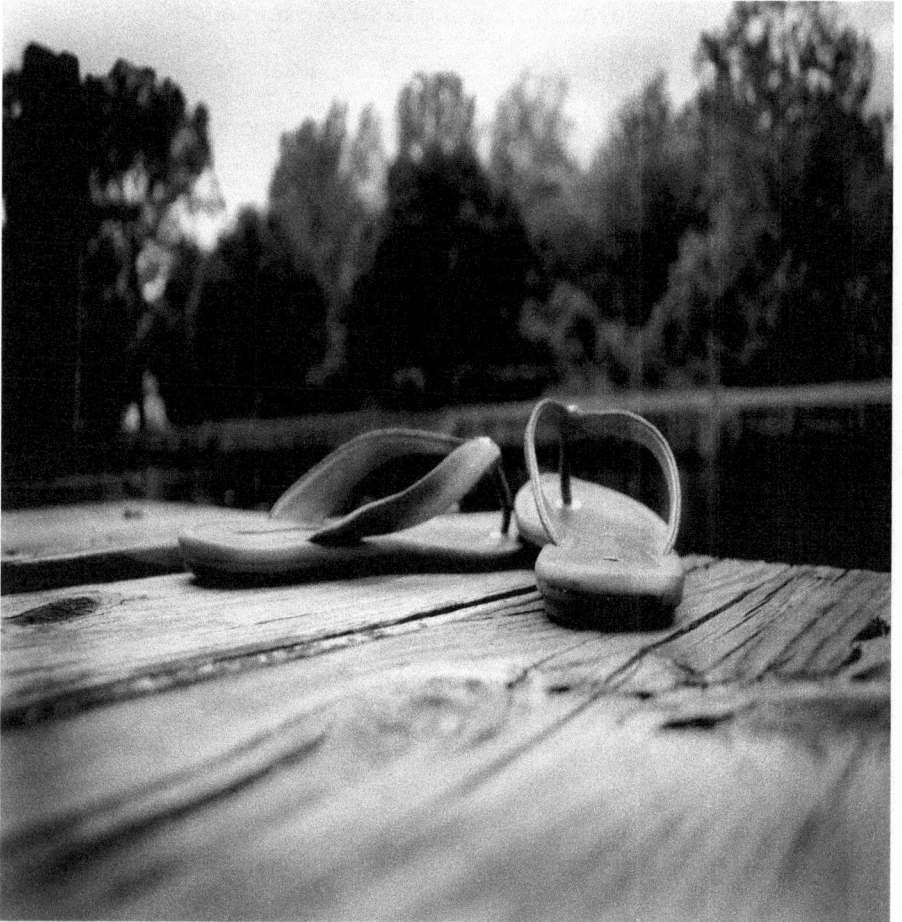

JERRY D. HAYES

Lives in Myrtle Beach, South Carolina- The Father of four wonderful children. Tara, Melissa, Jeremy and Jordan Hayes.

"Pablito" Inspired by Pablo Neruda's universal appeal to the beauty of a woman. "Pablito es la máscara poética que llevo".

PoetPablito@yahoo.com

www.ingramcontent.com/pod-product-compliance
Lightning Source LLC
Chambersburg PA
CBHW071018040426
42443CB00007B/835